Dating Smart

9 Tips to Transform Your *CRAZY* Dating Life

Linda D. Lowe

DATING SMART: 9 TIPS TO TRANSFORM YOUR *CRAZY* DATING LIFE.

Copyright © 2015 by Linda D. Lowe

This title is also available as an Amazon Kindle e-book (workbook not included).

www.LindaDLowe.com

All rights reserved. No part of this publication may be reproduced, stored in a retrieval system, or transmitted in any form, or by any method - electronic, mechanical, photocopy, recording, or any other - except for brief quotations embodied in critical articles or reviews, without prior permission of the author.

ISBN-13: 978-0692519783

DEDICATION

To Danielle:
May you date smarter than I did and understand the purpose of dating.
May you seek God, obey God, and live for God daily in all that you do.
Love Mommy

CONTENTS

Acknowledgments	vii
Prelude: The Search	9
Introduction: Bye CRAZY	17
Tip #1: Fix Yourself First	19
Tip #2: Create Your List	27
Tip #3: Become Friends	37
Tip #4: Beware of Flirting and Flirters	43
Tip #5: Get A Life	47
Tip #6: Cancel Your Benefits	55
Tip #7: Practice Purity	63
Tip #8: Discover Your Coach	69
Tip #9: From Date to Mate	77
Bonus Tip: Marriage	85
Conclusion: Hello New Me	89
Appendix 1: My List	95
Appendix 2: Me, Myself & I	97
Workbook: 90 Day Transformation	99

ACKNOWLEDGMENTS

Thanks to my team of young adult readers (Trish Angall, Christopher White, and Jonathan Copeland), my editor (Reneé Campbell) for enduring with me through ALL my adds, and ALL my friends for their encouragement and feedback when I needed it the most.

Prelude

| The Search |

The gentle breeze from the warm summer air made the evening more romantic as Sean and Shelley sat out on Sean's rooftop terrace underneath the moonlight celebrating their one year anniversary. Moments like these compelled Shelley to stay with Sean. He knew how to romance her right.

"Dinner was delicious as expected bae," Shelley complimented Sean for the third time that evening as she collected the dishes in order to head back inside.

"Thanks! You know I love cooking for you and putting a smile on your face. That makes me happy. I'ma make you my wife one day," Sean exclaimed as they walked down the stairs and into the kitchen.

Shelley smiled as the word *wife* rolled off his tongue. Behind her smile, though was everything but happiness and excitement. Sure, one day she wanted to be married but not to Sean. She just didn't know how to tell him yet.

* * *

Shelley and Sean cuddled up on the oversize chair

after washing and putting away the dishes. Sean couldn't stand a dirty kitchen; therefore, he made sure to clean it every night following dinner.

They watched their favorite movie while finishing up their Peach Cobbler pie Shelley baked from scratch earlier. Although she was loving the evening, she couldn't help but think of the growing discomfort she felt in their relationship.

The pain of their frequent verbal altercations, over Shelley's decision not to have sex, lingered in her mind longer than she wanted it to. The last altercation was by far the worst.

Sean's words pierced like thousands of needles forcing their way into her petite body. However, the pain didn't stop Shelley from firing back with her own insults and hateful words.

She had never been in so many intense verbal altercations in her life until she started dating Sean.

In order to drown her pain that night she took a couple of shots, for the first time in her life, of the Absolut Sean kept in stock. She eventually passed out on his living room floor, waking up the next morning in the same spot to a pounding headache. She wasn't sure if the headache was from the argument or the liquor, however she swore never to drink again.

Despite the severity of the argument, Sean nursed her back to health and acted as if the argument had never happened. His dysfunction was like the changing wind. One moment he was lovey dovey and the next he was a raging inferno.

Shelley decided to break off their relationship as she had done several times before, but she felt constant uneasiness since adjusting to the dysfunctional way of operating.

Sean too felt an uneasiness and void whenever Shelley would break off their relationship. As always he called her numerous times leaving several voice messages and sending multiple text messages. He recognized that he had gone too far this time and needed Shelley back. To show his remorse for his actions, he decided to take her to Hawaii for a week and Shelley decided to go.

Since returning, their relationship was a lot more calm. Sean now appeared as if he respected Shelley's decision to stop having sex. He no longer brought it up or attempted to convince her otherwise.

In fact, Sean continued to apologize for blowing up on her that night.

It had been exactly one month since they had sex, and although they were celebrating their one year dating anniversary Shelley had no intentions to renege. She was determined to keep her body in check that night even though it was screaming for Sean's.

She had slipped up a few times, well a lot of times, but this time she would be firm. She was tired of just sleeping with a guy that she already knew she wasn't going to marry.

"You nailed this pie Shelley," Sean said shaking his head in affirmation while finishing up his pie.

"I know right?!?!" Shelley responded with surprise in her voice.

"Do you want another piece?" Sean asked as he rose to his feet.

"Please. Thanks!" Shelley smiled as she handed him her plate. "Two scoops of ice cream please."

She watched intensely as he walked towards the kitchen and out of sight in his grey boxer briefs and white tee shirt.

"God help me. I really want him but I can't. I vowed to you that I wouldn't anymore and I'm sticking to it."

Shelley focused back on the movie and waited for Sean to return.

"What's taking so long?" Shelley yelled as she curled up under her pink throw blanket she kept at Sean's place.

Just as Shelley completed her question Sean reappeared carrying their second serving of pie in his right hand and his favorite after meal mix drink - Vodka and orange juice - in his left. This was his third round for the night. His usual was one.

Early into their relationship Shelley tried to convince him to stop drinking, but to no avail she couldn't. She realized that it led to more arguments and a waste of her breath.

He had been drinking since the age of sixteen; and now it was part of his evening routine. Shelley no longer fought against it but only accepted it.

"Do you want to have a drink with me tonight?" Sean asked taking a sip of his drink then placing it up to Shelley's lips.

"Do I drink with you any other night?" Shelley sarcastically responded gradually moving her head back.

"It's a special night though," Sean retorted moving the glass even closer to Shelley's lips.

Shelley continued to move her head back as far as it would go.

"Is that your decoy for getting me to have sex with you Sean?"

"I don't need a decoy. I know all your spots," Sean whispered in Shelley's ear planting a quick kiss on her cheek.

She took a deep breath and readjusted her position a few times clenching the blanket more tightly. Sean giggled and Shelley took another deep breath. She felt like the urge was about to jump right out of her and onto Sean's lap. *Not tonight* she thought to herself.

Sean pulled her closer to him causing Shelley more discomfort. Since he wasn't trying to make a move on her, she stayed there and cuddled but the urge only grew.

She removed the covers and sat Indian style, then she shifted into child pose, next she adjusted her legs over the arm. Every which way she moved the urge of sex grew stronger.

"Are you ok?" Sean asked.

"Yeah just trying to get comfortable. I think I'ma go sit in the other chair." Shelley proceeded to get up and walk across the room where the other chair was positioned; but Sean pulled her back down.

"Why do you need to go sit over there? We are celebrating our anniversary. At least cuddle with me! Are you sure you're ok?" Sean was aware that Shelley was aroused with all the fidgeting she was doing. He watched her as she fidgeted more. Sean got up, sat behind Shelley and started massaging her shoulders. All she could do was close her eyes.

"Come on bae. Just tonight." He whispered in her ear. "It's our anniversary. We can end the night with a BANG!" He shouted and jolted his body gently against hers.

He kissed Shelley down her neck and onto her left arm. Things were getting heated pretty fast. Shelley's body was screaming *YES* but her mind was screaming *NO*. She really wanted Sean but she really didn't want to have any regrets like before. She had promised God that she would wait.

"No Sean. I..I...I can't," she stuttered quickly pushing Sean away and rising from the chair. Sean gave Shelley an infuriated stare as he got up snatching his empty glass from the floor. He stomped to the kitchen with the blanket draped over his right shoulder, adjusting his boxers.

Shelley sat back down, threw her head back and gazed at the ceiling. "God help me." She closed her eyes and relaxed taking deep breaths.

Minutes later she heard Sean walking back into the room. Still relaxing, the song from the movie, that they had longed stopped watching, caught her attention. It was the song that she and John (her high school sweetheart and son's father) danced to at prom. She replayed the memory in her mind.

Suddenly she felt the splash of a cold liquid hitting her forehead and trickling down through her hair. She jumped up to see Sean bending behind the chair with his fourth drink raised in the air directly over the chair back where her head was resting.

"Really Sean! You're that upset with me that you would dump your drink on me?" Shelley shouted as loud as possible. Sean looked at Shelley with a frown and slight smirk.

Shelley figured that Sean intentionally splattered his drink in her face and hair because she would not have sex with him. This made her furious.

She lunged her 4'11", 100lb petite body over the chair jumping onto Sean's back hitting him profusely.

"You know I just got my hair done," she yelled.

Sean's drink fell to the carpeted floor. He swung her off his back into the chair. Shelley quickly popped back up and pushed Sean with all her might causing him to hit his back on the corner of the fireplace mantel.

She continued to pursue Sean swinging her arms out of control hitting him in his face. Sean grabbed Shelley's arms in the attempt to constrain her, but she continued to swing wildly.

"Calm down Shelley," Sean bellowed trying to catch his balance. Being tipsy didn't help.

Shelley continued to swing. Hit after hit, blow after blow straight to Sean's face. She cursed him, she spat on him and she kicked him.

Sean swiftly snatched Shelley's swinging arms as he moved away from the fireplace, but Shelley was still trying to swing.

Suddenly she fell to the floor kicking and screaming. Sean still had hold of her arms cursing and screaming at her. The two were not just engaged in a verbal altercation but physical too.

He dragged her across the room, into the kitchen, into the formal living room, to the front door and down the concrete steps of the front porch.

He left her there lying at the bottom of the stairs, in pain, crying and screaming.

Shelley had no energy left to try and run after him as he made his way back up the stairs, into the house, slamming the door behind him.

With her head in her hands she cried harder. Although no sound was coming out she could hear herself gasping for air.

Sean popped back out bringing her belongings. He ignored her as if she wasn't even there. He neatly placed her bags, clothes, shoes and other items she had stored at his house, at the curb. Then he made his way back into the house never to come out again.

Every verbal altercation they had flooded her memory. This one was the worst. *How could I not see this day coming?* She thought. *I should have never accepted him back the last time. I should have never took him back after he cussed me out the first time. What am I searching for?*

Shelley could not believe that she was just fighting the guy that claimed he wanted to marry her and always professed how much he loved her. The guy that she dated and had grown comfortable with.

Now she stood on the curb with no way home. She had thoughts of going back and asking Sean for a ride. She had thoughts of being lonely and missing the romance that he was so good at giving. She had thoughts of bitterness, anger and resentment.

Tears streamed down her face and snot flowed from her nostrils. She rummaged through her bags searching for her phone. Instead, she found the steak knife that she used earlier that evening at dinner.

She gripped the knife tightly in her hand as she stood beside Sean's car contemplating slashing all four of his tires and busting out every window possible.

Her body shook from the midnight breeze and her mind raced with rage. She gripped the knife tighter ready to remove it from the bag, but suddenly she felt her phone vibrate on her hand breaking her train of rage. She released the knife and retrieved her phone.

"Hello," she answered through sniffles and tears. It was Tee. "Come get me. This is *CRAZY*!!!"

Introduction

Bye CRAZY

*D*ating can be *CRAZY*! Whether you find yourself in a similar situation as my fictional characters, Shelley and Sean, or not.

I'm sure you may have your own crazy stories. If you don't have any crazy stories then try to keep it like that. I promise you I wouldn't want you to have to go through what Shelley and Sean went through or anything close to it.

Sometimes we set ourselves up in relationships and we can't even see it until something traumatic or heartbreaking takes place. We try to hold on to relationships we know we should let go of, or try to win people over that show very little to no interest in us. We see the signs but we ignore them only to regret it later.

Dating is about getting to know someone new not gaining a crazy ex or a *chip* on our shoulder.

Dating is about being yourself not putting on a façade in order to impress someone.

As a single female myself, I am long past trying to portray a persona that is false or gaining another story from another crazy relationship.

Too often I hear people in relationships say, "they weren't like that when we first met", or "they changed". They were either putting on a front or you just didn't want to notice who they really were because you were tired of being lonely.

After personal experience and biblical research, I've discovered a few things on dating that has changed my life. My discoveries will also change your life. They will leave you satisfied, fulfilled, and content. No more hopping from relationship to relationship or crazy to crazy.

Ditch the drama that too often comes with dating today and seek clarity.

Stop dating the same way expecting different results. Look at dating in a new light. So, don't put your claws into that person you got your eye on too quickly.

Ladies get your girls and guys rally up your boys, and read these 9 tips in a group. What you are about to read will spark a discussion.

It's not the battle of the sexes or about who is right or who is wrong.

These tips will challenge you, open your eyes, and set you on a better path when dating.

This isn't just a book to read but also a workbook. At the end of each tip you will find the *NOTE* page. Record your goals, feelings, etc. there. At the very end you will find the 90 Day Transform project with details.

Just to let you know. I define dating as two people exclusively in a relationship; therefore, I use dating and relationship interchangeably.

Are you ready to dig in?

Let's go!

Tip #1

FIX YOURSELF FIRST

I often hear singles talk about what they want in a man or woman, but too often lack those same things that they are requesting. Girl, yes you! Dude you too!

A single woman would say something like *"I want a man with money"* when she doesn't have a job herself. A single man would say *"I want a woman with a banging body"* when his body is banged up. Now, this isn't all single people but you understand what I'm saying.

Ladies, if you are requiring a man with money ideally you should have a job as well.

Guys, if you are requiring a woman's body to be nicely curved and trimmed in all the right places, then you must make sure that your body is chiseled and tapered in all the right places too. Keep it tight, *aight?*

We often search for requirements in a relationship that we want but have not achieved ourselves. We live vicariously through our partner thinking that since we are in a relationship with someone that has achieved these things then we don't have to.

Fix yourself first by becoming the person that you would want to date.

I know you are thinking that you are all of that and you very well may be - to yourself and your mommy that is. I know this may be a shocker to you but I'm sure there are some things about yourself that you can work on. In fact, we can all use some alterations and improvements no matter our age, level of education, or income.

Now, I don't want you to think that I'm saying the only reason you are not married is because there is something wrong with you. NO, I am NOT saying that at all. **Even married people have things that they need to fix about themselves.** What I am saying is we all have things that we need to fix about ourselves.

Have you ever conducted a self-evaluation? If not then you should. It's a good way to help you improve as a person.

Do a brief one now. Answer these questions honestly. That's the only way it will work. Once you have answered the questions ask your closest friend to answer those same questions about you. If they are your closest friend, then I expect that they will be honest with you as well as provide you with some great tips for helping you improve your character. Ok, here are the questions:

- *Are you easily angered? Explain.*
- *Do you provoke people? Explain.*
- *Are you forgiving? Explain.*
- *Are you spiteful? Explain.*
- *Are you selfish? Explain.*
- *Are you broken from past relationships? Including family relationships (past and present), friendships and dating relationships. Explain*

Use this space to record your responses.

These questions are important in a relationship because you must know how to control your anger instead of saying or doing things that you will regret later. You will need to know how to forgive even if you decide to break it off with the other person. You will need to be selfless as opposed to selfish.

If you are only concerned about the other person fulfilling your wants and doing things your way, chances are you want to date and marry yourself.

You must remember that being willing to address your own character flaws will determine the success of your marriage.

We often only see what's wrong with the other person and overlook our own detrimental characteristics.

I have used these questions during my own self-evaluations not just for a relationship but to improve myself overall.

These questions are just a foundation for you to build on. Add more specific questions as they relate to your life and development, such as: *How important is your relationship with God?* Create your own self-evaluation, similar to these questions. Write the questions and your answers every six months on a sheet of paper. Retain that information in order to review it at your next self-evaluation.

The goal of a self-evaluation is to reveal your current personality by allowing you to see it written down and help you recognize areas for improvement.

Compare your self-evaluation with how Christ calls us to Christian living. What does He say about anger? What does He say about forgiveness? Does your self-evaluation matchup? If not, don't be discouraged. Set goals for improvement.

Don't depend on anyone else to give you what you can and should achieve yourself. Adopt a healthy lifestyle, save more money (so that you can have more money), get the degree you want. When you get into that relationship and that person has those things that you like, it will only enhance your relationship.

Fixing yourself first is important to a healthy dating relationship but more importantly a healthy you.

Have you encountered some rough relationships that have left you broken, bruised and mad at men or women?

Are you going into new relationships projecting your anger onto that person for what your ex did?

Are you infuriated at your baby daddy or baby mama? Perhaps they ditched you to raise the child all by yourself.

There may be a lot more fixing you need to address immediately. Every pain, hurt or issue we've experienced from past relationships may need more than a self-evaluation. It may need you taking the time to seek help. If you don't, your dating life will always be crazy and chances are so will your married life.

Fixing yourself first sometimes requires us to dig deep in order to heal the pain that lies beneath the surface deep down in our core.

Fixing yourself first is also about learning what it takes to maintain a healthy, godly relationship. Start attending marriage seminars, reading marriage books (I recommend *Blueprints For Marriage* by Johnny Parker and *The 5 Love Languages: The Secrets to Love that Lasts* by Gary Chapman), listening to marriage podcasts and such.

The purpose for dating is to move towards marriage. If marriage is not your goal then there is no need to date. You just need friends to hang out with.

Let me explain.

DON'T date someone that is not interested in getting married. That is a SET UP for a meltdown. All that will produce are crying nights, stalking exes, and

CRAZINESS. If she or he has already expressed to you that they are not interested in marriage, that is your cue to leave.

I know what you are thinking and you need to stop it. NO, you CANNOT change their mind. NO, having sex with them or buying them a gift won't change their mind either. If they are not interested in eventually being married one day then you should not date them.

If they do decide to change their mind later then so be it, but don't wait around for them to do so. **Boy (girl) BYE!**

So, as I was saying before. It's important to educate yourself about marriage. This will begin to paint a picture of what marriage is really about.

A marriage doesn't last just because the sex is good or just because you look good or your spouse looks good. Sex is a benefit and good looks are dependent upon how well you keep yourself.

A solid marriage is built on God and the wisdom He offers through various means.

Befriend godly, married couples and listen to their advice. They will let you know the real deal. They will let you know that they don't always get along. They don't always like each other or they don't always agree. They will also let you know that they decided to work things out even when it got rough and believe me it gets rough.

You don't have to be married to know that but know this, effective communication is key to all healthy relationships and studies show that men and women communicate differently.

Do you know how to communicate effectively?

Be sure to **fix yourself first.**

|NOTES|

Tip #2

|CREATE YOUR LIST|

*Y*ou may have heard that as a Christian you shouldn't have a list, and only trust in God. As a Christian I've found out that having a list is a must, and trusting in God is a prerequisite. So, don't get rid of your list just tweak it.

Guys, I'm sure you are thinking that lists are for girls. Well, that's not the case. *Forreal, forreal,* we all have a list be it written down or stored in our memory. We all start somewhere, and too often the problem with singles isn't the people we date but the expectations on that list that we have.

Google defines expectation as "a strong belief that something will happen or be the case in the future." When our expectations aren't met we become irritated or even angry. You may expect to be married by a certain age, date the "perfect" person that will follow your every command, eat out at least three times a week, have walks on the beach with your date, etc. These are all expectations that you may be projecting onto someone that does not share the same expectations.

Do you know what I want you to do with those expectations? I want you to discard them. Yes! **Let go of those timelines and fantasies that you've created between you and yourself.** Understand that in a relationship it takes two people to communicate and agree how they will operate together, not one.

More times than often when we set our expectations it's not with the other person in mind. Now, if you were dating yourself then you would be able to fulfill each and every one of your expectations as you wished with no problem. Right? Of course! But you're not dating yourself, and if you are reading this book then I don't think you want to date yourself.

Now, discarding certain expectations doesn't mean that you will date any Joe blow or any Sue hoe. Instead it means that you will create a realistic list with God directing you as to what to place on that list. I call it the "Godlistic" list (God + realistic...what God wants for you).

The Godlistic lists consists of character traits that God has outlined for you. Many of these traits you can find in the Bible in people such as Ruth, Joseph, etc. Therefore, you will need to read your Bible more. That's why I call it "Godlistic".

You must rethink your list and take away some attributes while adding others. Avoid making these things concrete on your list: height, weight, hair length, money, and all of the non-character traits. These are preferences that will and can fluctuate. People can make lots of money one day and lose it the next.

Instead, your list should include character traits that create a solid foundation for a lasting relationship. Things such as: trustworthiness, faithfulness, commitment, and honesty. A person with these traits promotes a great dating relationship, and evolves into a great spouse and overall a great friend worth keeping.

Speaking of friend, don't disregard the importance of being friends when dating and when married. Establishing a genuine friendship allows an atmosphere of comfort and openness while dating and within marriage.

As a person that values genuine friendships, I need to know that my husband is my friend. I need to know that my husband isn't going to lie to me. I need to know that above all he is faithful to God in good and bad times. This lets me know that if he is faithful to God, then he will be faithful to his godly role as a husband. I don't need him to jump ship just because waves are rocking the boat and water is gushing in. I need him to be committed by sticking it out and working through it.

Isn't that what you would want to know about your spouse too?

See, marriage isn't only love. It encompasses friendships and commitments too. Like Tina Turner said, "What's love got to do with it?" Not a DANG thing when he or she aint committed.

Another important attribute that should make up your list is personality traits. These are attributes that you can connect with. Their personality must be one that compliments yours; i.e. you have to like their personality.

I personally like to be sarcastic; therefore, I need someone that has a sense of humor as well as understands my sarcasm. If a guy doesn't like sarcasm then I know I wouldn't date him, and I'm sure he wouldn't date me. Pretty simple right? Yeah, I think so.

Personality traits are things such as: How does this person approach situations? Are they aggressive or passive? Are they an introvert or extrovert? Are they soft spoken or loud? Do they like to be the center of attention or low key?

If all the person got going for themselves are money and looks but you don't like their personality traits, be sure not to date them. Their personality traits aren't going to change much.

Physical appearance is another thing that should be included on your list. Yes, physical appearance is something that can change and it will change over time. This is why I placed it here and not at the top. It's important though that you are physically attracted to the person that you are in a relationship with. Remember that beauty is in the eye of the beholder; therefore, you don't have to behold someone you're not attracted too.

I know sometimes we try to go after that person that everybody thinks is fine, but this is a time to block everyone else out. When it comes to your relationship and the physical features of that person you are dating, that is solely up to you.

Be with someone who you find attractive physically, intellectually, socially, spiritually, and on all levels. Your family members don't have to think that they are attractive nor do your friends; just as long as you do.

Ask God to help you compile a "Godlistic" list. Write it down, place the date on it and save it. Alter it as much as you need to; make it as detailed as you want.

Remember, this list is your guide to choosing a date wisely, therefore discernment is needed as well as reading your Bible.

Here are a few people you should look up for character traits: Ruth (she has her own book), Joseph (Genesis chapter 37-50), Mary (the mother of Jesus. Luke 1:27 - and keep reading), and Stephen (Acts chapter 6 and 7).

Your list is to help you understand what you want in

a person, and to keep you focused. Don't keep dating those persons that disrespect you and run over you. If you do then pay tip #1 another visit.

Ask God to reveal to you what needs to be on your list.

Want to know what my list looks like? Take a peek at Appendix 1 after you finish reading this section.

Write your own list here.

Now that you have taken time to write out your list, I want you to write a second list. I call the second list "Me, Myself and I". On this list you will write out what you want for yourself; your standards, your boundaries, your deal breakers, and so on. This list outlines guidance for yourself; therefore, you will need to hold yourself accountable to this list (or find an accountability partner).

I realized in my earlier 20's that I was dating all wrong. My goal was to be with somebody just for the sake of having somebody. I didn't have any real concrete standards, guidelines, or boundaries.

Have you every dated like that before? Are you still dating like that?

I was in a relationship for a year. I knew that relationship was all wrong for me. When I decided to get out of that relationship, I immediately set standards for myself. I was determined that I would not have sex anymore until I was married or be with someone that pressured me to have sex, that I would not go out with a guy if I knew for sure that it wasn't going to go anywhere, and that I would not date just because I had nothing else to do. So what if he was FINE. If he had an anger issue then no I'm not interested in dating him. So what if he drove a nice car and had money, but disrespected me and always said it was a joke.

Sometimes we will date people just to get out of the house. That's not dating smart. That's lacking friendships.

Set your standards before the date, stick to them and communicate them to the one you are dating.

There are some things on your list that may be negotiable, but be sure to know the difference of the negotiable standards and the non-negotiable standards. You can find my "Me, Myself and I" list in Appendix 2.

Write your "Me, Myself and I" list here.

Your list is your foundation. It helps you understand what you will allow or not allow. **Remember that we (whether verbal or non-verbal) teach people how to treat us.**

In school, did you have a teacher that practically allowed you or other's to breeze through their class? If the homework wasn't completed on time they allowed, almost always, extensions.

On the other hand I'm sure you also had that no non-sense teacher that, almost always, never allowed extensions. You always did their work first. Right?

Do you know why you approached the two differently? (And it doesn't have anything to do with if they were nice or not.) You approached the two differently because they communicated (either verbally or non-verbally) their standards to you. Perhaps the no non-sense teacher didn't accept your late assignment and the other teacher did.

So, if you want someone to treat you a certain way be sure to communicate that information to them. Don't leave them guessing. Don't assume that they already know how to treat you if you haven't told them. NO ladies, men are not mind readers and neither are women. It doesn't work like that. If you want them to know then tell them by using your words. If you don't appreciate them yelling at you then tell them. If they cannot respect your standards and boundaries then be out.

Your list will include both negotiables and non-negotiables. If a person doesn't have every single thing on your list of negotiables, then don't make a big deal of it. It could be because they are still growing. I'd rather be with someone who is willing to grow, than to be with someone that is stuck in their ways. It could also be because this is who they are. If it's not a deal breaker then deal with it.

However, if they don't have your non-negotiables and

don't respect them then they are not worth your time. Believe me there is someone out there that will respect, honor and treat you with dignity.

Create your list and stick to it!

| NOTES |

Tip #3

| BECOME FRIENDS |

I briefly mentioned establishing a genuine friendship under tip #2 Create Your List. True friendships are investments yielding a return tremendously benefiting both persons involved.

Establish a friendship before a dating relationship. In order to become friends before dating you MUST allow the relationship to naturally evolve and not rush into dating too soon.

When I first met the few people who are now my closest friends, we didn't necessarily talk every day or hang out every day. Yes, being in college or attending the same church placed us in the same proximity often but not always. Our relationship started out as acquaintances. We would hang out some days and other days we didn't. As we realized that we had similarities and some of the same interests, we hung out more. Naturally our relationship moved from acquaintance to friendship.

What I'm saying is don't force getting to know each other. You don't see people walking around that just met someone saying, "Oh I need to be with them every day so our friendship will grow."

When we meet someone we are physically attracted to, our first inclination is to date them. When we discover that they have more characteristics that we like, we want to date them even more.

Just because we may find them physically attractive or even like their personality doesn't mean that we have to date them immediately or at all. This rapid cycle leads us seeking to connect on a deeper level way too soon.

When trying to establish a genuine friendship you don't want to connect too deep too fast because **if you need to get out, you want to be able to do that without damage being done.**

If you feel like the other person is moving too fast let them know. Don't avoid them, that only makes them press you harder.

On the other hand, don't be fearful of moving slow because you think they will fall for someone else if ya'll aren't always talking or together. If they do fall for someone else then know that this person is no longer interested in you. Not only are they no longer interested in you, but they aren't someone you would want to be with or waste your time on.

I HATE hearing girls say, *she stole my man*. Nah, boo boo. He wasn't yours! More so, he's not a man that you would want to be with in the long run. Let him go.

We can't make someone like us or be with us if they have already decided that they are not interested.

Too often singles spend their time and energy chasing someone that is not interested in a relationship with them. They think that if they talk to them more frequently or hang around them more often than eventually the other person will "fall" for them. They attempt to force a friendship and/or relationship on the other person.

Guys will try to buy the lady and ladies will try to lure the guy with sex. In the end they both get played.

Guys, trying to buy a lady will never keep her your lady. She will only stick around as long as the money continues to flow or until she finds someone else with more money.

Ladies, connecting with sex will not keep the guy interested in you, so don't give up the cookies when dating. Have you ever heard the saying: why buy the cow when the milk is free? **Don't give your milk or cookies away for free**. Wait until you are married.

So, let me go deeper into the sex thing. Once sex is introduced into a dating relationship it will cloud your decision-making. Note that sex is the glue that binds the two together.

What does this mean? Simple! What you would not have tolerated before sex becomes tolerable after sex. Yes, it is true. I talk more about this topic under Tip #6 Cancel Your Benefits.

So, in order to establish a genuine friendship leave sex out along with other forms of physical touch that sexually arouse you and them.

Becoming friends first creates a sturdy foundation for a relationship. When a friendship naturally develops over time two people appreciate and value each other more.

Be informed though that every person you are attracted to should not lead to a date or a friendship, and there is nothing wrong with that.

Becoming friends though before dating allows you to weed out unnecessary relationships.

After ya'll have established a genuine friendship then talk about the possibility of a relationship and move accordingly. Just make sure the other person is on the same page as you.

How many people would you have avoided being in a relationship with if you had established a friendship with them first?

I met many people in college. All of them are not my close friends today. Some are in my networking circle, others are acquaintances, and some I have not been in contact with since leaving college. Out of the hundreds of people that I met in undergrad and grad school and the groups that I rolled with, only three people today are my closest friends. This isn't because the others and I had a falling out, but because we did not naturally evolve as long term friends, and that's ok.

Every guy or girl you meet, everyone that flirts with you or you think is attractive isn't meant for you to become friends with, and that's ok.

Every person of the opposite sex that you become friends with isn't meant for you to date or be in a relationship with and that's ok too.

Now, I'm not saying that ya'll will be enemies because you shouldn't be that either. You may establish a networking relationship or never communicate again.

There are only so many close friends that we will have. This is why it is so important not to force getting to know someone or to have sex with them. We either naturally grow apart or naturally grow closer. When you and the person you are establishing a friendship with naturally grow apart, you should be able to part without feeling guilty, stuck or awkward.

On the contrary, when you naturally grow closer you should not feel forced, discomfort or like the friendship is a fake. Start out as friends with no pressure to see or talk to each other excessively. See what develops when you take things at a pace that is not rushed.

Become friends first.

|NOTES|

Tip #4

BEWARE OF FLIRTING AND FLIRTERS

*T*here are different levels of flirting. I like to categorize these levels as: green light flirting; yellow light flirting; and red light flirting.

Green light flirting is letting one know that you are interested in them. The flirtee responds to the green light flirt by stopping it with a shutdown or driving it with their own green light flirt (e.g. "Can I take you out?"). Green light flirting signals interest in getting to know one's character and personality.

Yellow light flirting signals connection and attraction not necessarily sexual. At this level both persons say, "I like being around you. Can we have more of these times?"

Red light flirting signals sex. The person flirting on this level is straightforward with their message be it verbal or non-verbal. Either way you know that they are there for sex if nothing else.

A person that is after you for sex lives in the red light district. Why? Because they are straight freaks. And

I'm not talking about weird. I'm referring to the freaks in the bedroom. Their intention is sex, sex and more sex. With these three levels of flirting it is up to the flirtee to stop the flirting or drive it.

Other flirters are subtle and will reel you in starting in the green light district, and before you know it you're swinging from a pole and spending all your money. Well, some of you anyway.

Ladies, when a guy we think is attractive flirts with us it heightens our awareness that he is feeling us. Therefore, we walk sexier to make him pay attention to us even more. When a girl flirts with a guy it does the same thing for him. Just be aware of how they are flirting and how you respond.

Flirting can sometimes be harmless but it also can be harmful. As people we want to be wanted by others. We wanted to know that our parents wanted us, that our siblings wanted us, that as we grow that our future spouse want us.

To be wanted is natural, but you must know that being desperate to have someone want you is not. If you are desperate for attention from the opposite sex then you must ask yourself *what am I lacking in my life?* (A husband/wife is not the answer, sorry.)

How do you know that you are being desperate? You do anything just to keep them around even if you are uncomfortable with it. If you are desperate you most likely lack genuine healthy friendships with others and/or there is a void from your family structure that you are trying to fulfill.

Let me pause again to debunk some possible foolishness that you were taught to believe. Ladies, we need other ladies as friends. If you have had bad experiences with female friends then keep searching. If you feel like you keep attracting foolish female friends then take a look at yourself. We attract who we are.

Guys, you also need other guys as friends. They help you develop as men.

So, back to what I was mentioning about being desperate. Another indication that you could be desperate is if your relationship with God is lacking. All these things and more can cause you to be desperate. **A desperate person is never worth dating.** So, if you were able to identify as a desperate person focus on strengthening yourself by building healthy friendships, restoring family relationships and connecting with God.

Remember this. Every person that flirts with you doesn't deserve your attention. Sometimes we are "fed" by filtering because we crave attention, affirmation and acceptance. If flirting is something that you need in order to feel better about yourself, then I recommend that you sit down with a professional to help you overcome a hurtful past.

If someone's flirting makes you uncomfortable shut it down. Remember, you must communicate your standards and boundaries. They are attempting to take you to that "red light district." Trust your instinct. That may mean you need to stop responding to their text messages or other messages. Do whatever you need to do to subtract yourself from a red light district flirt. It will save you from fornication.

Have you read the story of Joseph in Genesis chapter 39? Joseph is a prime example of shutting down a red light flirt. Take the time to read what he did. Even if you've read it before read it again. His approach is not dramatic but necessary to avoid fornication.

Beware of flirting and flirters.

|NOTES|

Tip #5

| GET A LIFE |

One Friday night I was bored out of my mind. It was an evening summer day. The weather was just right to be outside. Instead I was inside with nothing to do. I decided that I wanted to hang out with some friends, but everyone was busy. My phone rang, but I didn't recognize the number. Now usually if I don't recognize the number then I won't answer; however, this time I answered.

"Hello," I said in my professional voice since I did not recognize the number. (Yeah, you know how you switch up from work as opposed to at home or hanging out.)

The person on the other end greeted me back and began to ask how I was doing.

"I'm...fine," I responded hesitantly still trying to catch the voice.

"May I ask whom I'm speaking with?" I asked, again in my professional voice.

It was a guy I had not talked to in about five months. He was calling to see if I wanted to go out for a movie and a drink, then stay the night with him in his hotel. (His job sent him to my part of the state for the weekend. We lived approximately two hours apart.) I looked at the phone as if I was looking directly at him with the expression *boy please*.

I laughed out loud and said, "You know I don't drink and no I'm not spending the night with you."

"What about a movie?" he asked.

What about your baby mama that you live with and your youngest child that is fresh out of the womb, I thought.

His youngest child was less than a year old. When we first met he was upfront with informing me that he had two daughters that lived with him full-time, which I had no issue with, but it did raise concern. Where was their mother? I had never met a single dad whose children lived with him full-time. Now that's not to say there are no single dads out there whose children live with him full-time. I'm sure they are out there. However, I questioned him about her every chance I got and it eventually came out that they lived together. (I have the gift of interrogation.)

He claimed that they were no longer dating just living together. When I found this out I told him to stop calling me, and I immediately deleted his number from my phone. However, he had not done the same.

Here it was, months after I had cut him off; he was back on my phone.

Well, I told him to call me back later that evening and I would let him know what I was going to do. That was my way of turning him down nicely. That fool knew I wasn't going to go out with him that's why he never called me back.

I was bored but I wasn't stupid. I mixed my own fruity non-alcoholic drink, sipped on it that Friday night and mmmmm it hit the spot!

As much as I wanted to go out that night - and he presented me with the opportunity to do so - I would have been the fool if I had gone.

I wasn't going out with him even if it was just a "movie". I had more important things to do the next morning, commitments to fulfill, and great plans for my future. So, I wasn't going to get caught up in his trap. (*Spend the night with you in your hotel!* That's a red light district flirt.)

It's important that as a single person you have a life outside of dating. This includes having a clear vision of your goals be it career or personal.

Don't get caught up in traps just because you are bored. **Boredom can get you caught up, knocked up, and messed up.**

What's your hobby? Where do you like to volunteer? What are your future goals and what is your plan to get there? There are plenty of things you can do to keep your mind occupied instead of sitting around wishing that you were in a relationship or on a date.

If you are currently in college join a sports team or college club. If you are a young professional volunteer in your neighborhood or church. If you can afford it travel. Learn a new hobby or rekindle an old one. Find something that will impact your life and someone else's in a positive way and will keep your mind and time occupied.

One of the many things I enjoy doing as a single lady is hanging out with my family and hanging with my girls. We have movie nights, dinner nights, trips to the beach, and so on. I have many friends that I can hang out with during the week or on weekends. I love hanging out with my girls!

I also spend my time volunteering at church with the youth. I plan retreats, events, and preach.

I make sure that my daughter and I have our time together as well.

On top of that I run my own business. I'm a speaker, writer and a woman's life coach. I do have downtime to myself and relax with God, but I stay busy for a reason.

Occupy your time with productive things and stop spending it just thinking about being in a relationship. You will drive yourself to depression always wishing that you were in a relationship.

Singleness is a great time to travel, volunteer more, write a book, go to school, discover your purpose, and live out your purpose. I have done these very things as well as connected with God on a much deeper level. This isn't to say that you cannot do these things while you are married, but doing them as a single allows you to accomplish as much as you want while operating on your own schedule.

Have you ever heard the saying, "an idle mind is the devil's playground?" It is. How many times did or do you find yourself in a situation just because you had nothing else to do? Go hang out with friends and enjoy life.

Perhaps you may feel like you don't have any friends to hang out with because you live in a new city or new state. Get connected with your church or neighborhood groups and network. Don't limit yourself from networking with others. This is a good way to establish new friendships as well as business deals for you business-minded singles.

Stop viewing singleness as a curse and living your single life only to get married. Singleness is a blessing that many singles miss out on because they are so focused on finding a mate.

Singleness does not define who you are, just like marriage will not define who you are. In fact, the apostle Paul tells us that singleness is even better than marriage, but if you marry you are not sinning (1 Corinthians 7:8). Check out that entire chapter. It's good!

God ordained marriage and He is for marriages, but some people aren't ready. This includes some already married people. But anyway, **if we are not satisfied in our singleness then we will not be satisfied in our marriage.** So, whether married or single your life's focus should be to live for God. Don't live your single life to get married because once you get married will you stop living? I hope NOT.

* * *

Seeking God first instead of a relationship is dating smart. Many singles pray that God will send them a spouse, but few of those singles actually seek God for that spouse. Seeking God isn't just praying for Him to grant desires. Seeking God is searching for Him to fulfil His desire through your life.

How do you come to know God's desires for your life? You have to connect with God. This must be a daily ongoing conversation not just a hit and miss or a one night stand. Ask Him what plans He has for your life today. Tell Him your plans. See if they match up. Read God's Word daily so that you can get to know God and His plans for your life. **Make God your first priority and not just your matchmaker.**

When we seek God daily we are able to sync with Him and discover what He has for us, who he has for us, and when He will have them for us. We can't qualify people to be our spouse no matter how much we want that person. However, what we can do is genuinely enjoy our singleness and stop living like singleness is a plague.

I tend to notice that singles who do not have an active

life end up in relationships that they eventually don't want to be in and/or regret. They rush to hook up with someone thinking that it will cure their loneliness. These singles find themselves in and out of relationships more frequently than other singles that have an active life.

When I was in high school I knew people who had a different boyfriend or girlfriend every other month. When I got to college I realized that things didn't change much. The only difference were the people. Six years after graduating from grade school things are still the same just different people.

Do you know people like this? Are you that person?

Being in relationships have become their life and often times they have a lot of hurt, brokenness, bitterness, anger, and drama. These singles need a time-out from dating in order for God to restore them from broken, past relationships. They need a time-out from dating to understand who they are. They need a time-out from dating in order to receive healing. They need a time out from dating in order to build or rebuild their self-worth, self-confidence and self-esteem. (I'm working on my next book, *Time-Out: Connecting With God in my Singleness*. It depicts my life of singleness. Sign up for my email list so that when it's available you will be among the first to know. www.LindaDLowe.com)

I'm sure you may know some people like this or you may be that person. How do you know if you are this person? You've hopped into relationships back-to-back since you started dating. **Good news!** It's not too late to change your cycle.

Do you recall I mentioned volunteering and picking up a hobby a few paragraphs ago? In order to change your cycle of hopping from relationship to relationship incorporate activities in your life. Yeah, you might not be used to or like doing some things by yourself, but I promise you if you get a life you will discover more about who you are and you will begin to enjoy you.

Remember singleness is not a curse it's a blessing, so get a life and enjoy every moment!

|NOTES|

Tip #6

CANCEL YOUR BENEFITS

𝓑enefits are great when you are negotiating your benefits package at work, but not great for the dating package. Do you know why? See, **friends with benefits will soon become friends with deductibles.** Chi ching! (Yeah, go ahead and tweet that @LLivingthelife).

God made sex to connect the husband and wife on the physical, emotional, and spiritual levels. Therefore, keep this in mind: Sex is the glue that binds the two together forever. This works whether you're married or not. How many people have you connected with?

Premature sex destroys a relationship from truly developing. Once sex has entered the dating relationship it creates a fog or cloudiness that is difficult and at times impossible to see through.

Do you ever wonder why breaking up is so, so, so difficult after sex has been introduced in a dating relationship, as opposed to a dating relationship that does not include sex? You are basically leaving a part of yourself behind. It's like getting your arm caught in an elevator door, ripping the remainder of your body away in order to break free while leaving your arm in the door, and then you walk away as if everything is normal.

If you were in this situation your reaction would be to save your arm. Right? I hope so. You would work diligently at getting your arm out while still attached to your body. You would scream for help. You would try to pry the doors open. You would do all you can to free your arm and save it. Just thinking about having my arm stuck in an elevator door is painful.

In order to walk away from a dating relationship with all your *body parts attached*, leave sex out.

In 1 Corinthians 6:19 Paul, the author, states "flee fornication." The Greek word fornication is *porneia*. This is where the English word porn is derived. **Therefore, when we fornicate we are participating in porn.** Wow that sounds really bad! There are many everyday unpaid porn stars walking the college campus, sitting in their office with the great views or at their cubicle, and even in the church pews. Ouch, that may have hurt, but it is the truth. We view porn as a person having sex on camera, but porn is really just fornication.

When Paul says flee fornication, he doesn't just mean run from it but to seek safety from it. When someone seeks safety it means that they are currently in danger.

If I'm seeking safety from fornication then I don't just need to leave his house; I need to cut him off. I need to delete his number. I need to unfriend him on Facebook and unfollow him on Twitter, Instagram and Snapchat. I cannot seek safety from something but still stay connected. That's just taking a vacation.

Too many Christians only take vacations from fornication when they think that they are staying away from it.

When a drug addict seeks to break their drug addiction they (should) seek help through programs that help drug addicts break their addictions. They cut off their drug addict friends and such, and become part of a safe team of people that once were like them but now have been changed.

Don't just run from fornication with no safety net to run to. Connect with a safe person or a group of people that can help you overcome fornication. If you don't have a safe group of people to connect with then you need to really consider changing your circle of friends.

I once met this guy who told me he would not marry a woman without having sex with her first. He had been married before but was now divorced and told me that the sex was horrible. You know what? That was his fault. He should have taught his wife (now ex) what to do.

Do NOT believe that stupidity. You don't have to make sure the sex is good before marriage or that ya'll are "sexually compatible". You **TEACH** your spouse and you both learn along the way. (Team work produces fireworks. KABOOM!)

Well, he wasn't part of my safe group. Number deleted.

A safe group of people are people who have canceled their benefits and who are helping others to do the same. **It's possible. I know.** My benefits have been canceled for 12 years, and I have absolutely NO regrets. No, I'm not backed up and no, I'm not in need of some. In fact I'm filled with the Spirit which I need daily!

As I stated in tip #1, the purpose of dating is to get married where the two can enjoy the benefits of marriage. However, until marriage, sex benefits should not be included.

Another benefit that should not be included when dating is: living together or spending the night. Don't set yourself up. This helps defray from fornication. I know you say that you can control yourself and that may be true until your hormones kick into full force because of that movie or music you are watching or playing. Always err on the side of caution. The moment you think you are strong is the moment you will fall.

Perhaps you already live together. Well, it's never too late to move out. Living together is connecting too deep too fast. It provides a false sense of security in the relationship and it makes you dependent upon one another in ways that you should not have to be, such as financially.

One of the main reasons couples live together is because they want to save money. Well, it may help you save money but I promise you it will help you lose your connection with God too.

Living together will also convince you that you should stay in a relationship even if you want out. Let me explain.

You may realize that this person is not willing to marry you nor are they willing to adjust some of their unhealthy ways for the betterment of the relationship. You make excuses for staying. Excuses like: *I can't afford to live on my own. Where am I going to live?* You have now been convinced that you need this person in order to survive financially.

If this is you revisit tip #1.

Couples also decide to live together because they would rather play house instead of commit to marriage. They want all the benefits of marriage without the commitment of marriage. These are people you want to avoid like the plague.

Canceling your benefits means that you can't live together or spend the night because sex will happen.

Again, as a follower of Christ we should always live to

please Him. Really ask yourself is living together or spending the night worth risking a slip up? Sure, Christ forgives but we should never use His forgiveness as a back door policy for intentional sin. How would you respond if a person you knew intentionally caused you pain? They asked for your forgiveness and you forgave them continuously, but they continued to do the same thing and had no desire to change their actions or just made excuses for their actions. How sincere is their apology?

James 4:17 states (and I'm paraphrasing): *If you don't do what you know is right, you are sinning.*

Live in your own place and find time to spend with one another outside of a tempting situation. This doesn't just include each other's homes, but any space where you are more likely to be tempted.

You don't want to compromise your relationship with God. The body is the temple of the Holy Spirit. In other words, if we want the Holy Spirit to dwell there then no other spirits can.

You have heard of Sexually Transmitted Diseases (STDs), but have you heard of the Sexual Transference of Demons (STDs)? This is the lust demon seeking to trap us in all kinds of fornication. Once the doors are open for this demon to enter it controls us for as long as we yield and participate. This demon doesn't go away just because two people say "I do". It sticks around as long as it is entertained, nurtured, and allowed.

If fornication is practiced until marriage the chances of adultery increases substantially because the lust demon is still sticking around.

Whatever you feed will grow. People don't get fat because they don't eat and they don't get fat because they eat healthy. People get fat because they eat (most likely they overeat) and they eat unhealthy. Stop feeding the lust demon and start starving it. Start feeding the Holy Spirit in your life and feed it daily.

As I mentioned before, sex connects. The saying, *no strings attached* is a lie. So, married or not sex will do its job of connecting the two people. God says in the book of Genesis that the two became one flesh (Genesis 2:24). Becoming one flesh with your spouse is blessed by God. However, becoming one flesh with others is not. Therefore, not yielding to fornication is bigger than not getting pregnant or contracting a lifelong and/or deadly Sexually Transmitted Disease - as you know these are things that can likely occur. Not yielding to fornication is about not interrupting our connection with God.

Keep sex out and sleep and live in your own place. Now is the time to **cancel your benefits.**

NOTES

Tip #7

| PRACTICE PURITY |

"This movie is really putting me in the mood," Jay said to Natalie his fiancé of six months kissing her after every word. Jay had just graduated from law school ten months earlier and now was renting his first apartment. He had only been in his new place for two weeks. Each night he tried to convince Natalie to stay the night so that they could get a feel for what it would be like as a married couple. At first she said *no*, especially since she and Jay had decided that they wanted to wait until their honeymoon before they had sex again.

Natalie had an abortion three months earlier for the second time in their relationship. The first abortion was early on in their relationship. It was Natalie's idea and although she was remorseful she thought that it was best since she didn't know where their relationship was headed. In fact, Natalie never revealed to Jay that she was pregnant.

The second abortion was Jay's idea. He was halfway through law school and decided that neither one of them were ready. On the surface they both appeared healed from their decisions but deep down they weren't. They both regretted immensely the abortions. They were cuddled up on the floor enjoying their romantic candlelight dinner from their favorite pizza place. As irresistible as they were to each other and with their eyes fixed on the sex scene in the movie, Jay couldn't help but make his move. Their bodies were in sync, *feening* for one another.

"Wait Jay," Natalie whispered. "No sex," she said.

"I know. No sex. We can do other things," Jay responded. Natalie was all for other things.

I'm not just big on "no sex" before marriage; I'm big on purity in general and so is God.

Purity is being free from contamination. The culture we live in is loaded with sexual images **ALL the TIME**. We may not be able to avoid seeing that billboard as we drive down the street, but we can control what we watch on TV and in the movies. We can control what we decide to read in books and which websites we decided to browse, as well as the people we hang around.

There are singles that practice abstinence but do not practice purity. Some singles like to ask the question: "How far can I go without going too far?" Is that your question? Well, if that is your question then you are already setting yourself up to go too far. Your question should be: "How can I stay pure?" The answer to that is found in Psalm 119:9 - "By obeying your [God] word." A lot more simplistic than you thought, huh?

Obedience is crucial to us living a fulfilling and satisfying life.

As people we want to know our purpose and God's will for our lives. How would you feel if I told you that I know your purpose and God's will for your life? Yes, you. Do you want to know? I'm sure you do. This is the will of God for your life. Go to 1 Thessalonians 4:3. It states clearly God's exact will for your life. His will (and I'm paraphrasing) is that we stay away from sexual sin.

Guess what? **There is nothing sinful about sex or the desire for sex when in its proper element.** In fact it's natural to desire sex. I bet they didn't tell you that in church nor did your parents mention it when they talked to you – if they talked to you - about "the birds and the bees". (I hate that term. Call it what it is SEX. Ok, I digress). Since we naturally have a desire for sex we also must know how to manage that desire.

In 1 Corinthians 7:1 Paul mentions (and I'm paraphrasing) "It is not good for a man to touch a woman." This kind of touch he refers to is any form of sexual arousal which can be included but not limited to kissing and body massages. Yes, those massages from him or her feel real good but they can really get us into trouble.

Often times we try to make up for sex by doing other things such as foreplay or oral to say "at least I didn't have sex." But oral sex is sex, and anal sex is sex, and participating in either is not practicing purity.

God doesn't want us to not just have sex with a person that is not our spouse, but he wants us to be pure. Practicing purity helps us connect with Him more genuinely.

Have you ever felt like your connection with God was limited? Check your life and see if it's the lack of purity that is limiting you. **The more we yield to an impure lifestyle, the more limited we make ourselves to God.**

One day I had to preach a sermon. As I prepared that sermon God revealed something I thought was so profound. Have you ever asked God to give you more of

Him? Well, I have. In that moment God revealed that He doesn't give Himself in parts. In fact, He gives us all of Him. It's us that do not receive all of God because we actually give ourselves to Him in parts. It's not more of God we need. It's more of us that we need to give to God. We have to give God all of us in order to practice purity the way He wants us to.

Purity is a lifestyle not just a phase. What kind of places do you hang out at? Places where people are constantly reminding you of sex whether verbal or nonverbal? What kind of movies do you watch or books do you read or music do you listen to? A lot of books, movies and music portray sex, sex and more sex. Yeah, you may like the beat of that song but does it place your mind in a certain atmosphere? The movie may be funny and entertaining but does it make you want some afterwards? The book can be a page turner, but is it only talking about that person sleeping with him, her, and them? If you really want to practice purity you need to change the things you place in your mind.

When I became serious about practicing purity I started reading my Bible way more. I decided that I wouldn't watch movies with sex in it. That I wouldn't read those books that I loved so much by that author who really knew how to tell a captivating story. I stopped listening to certain music and stopped hanging around certain people. I became serious about practicing purity. I had to purge impure things that were keeping me back. If my daily life included watching sex or reading about sex, then I would no doubt have sex on my mind. What do you think?

Changing your lifestyle is a MUST in order to practice purity. It's so important that you guard what your eyes see, what your ears hear and what your mind absorbs.

Learning to practice purity in your singleness will

protect you from fornication and will equip you for practicing purity in your marriage. Yes, even in marriage you must practice purity. It's a lifestyle for a lifetime.

Don't think that just because you get married that you will automatically stop fornicating. Yes your sex will be "legal", but if you continue to practice fornication throughout your singleness that same mentality will follow you into your marriage.

Remember the lust demon I mentioned in the last tip? It follows you into your marriage. Why do you think there are so many husbands and wives cheating on their spouses? They are used to an active sex life with multiple people even if it is a few people. The lust demon includes fornication, pornography and such, and it will plague your marriage if you don't change your lifestyle.

If you haven't already committed yourself to a life of purity then now is the time. Start with these verses: 1 Thessalonians 4:3-8 and Ephesians 5:5-7. Also read the verses that I listed in this tip.

Practicing purity makes for a better dating life because you are able to give yourself fully to God!

|NOTES|

Tip #8

DISCOVER YOUR COACH

*E*very sports team has at least one coach. Coaches help athletes develop to their full potential and work towards achieving great success for the betterment of the athlete and the team at large. Coaches help athletes train in order to improve their skills, assess their performance, and encourage and motivate them.

The coach will play many different roles to the athlete such as instructor, mentor, friend, advisor, supporter, fact finder, counselor, fountain of knowledge, and much more.

Without a coach athletes will not develop or be challenged to become the best player that they can become. Honestly, without coaches sports would not be the lucrative, entertaining arena it is today. No player would be successful and no team would win because they would have no coach to teach them how to win.

The win in dating is marriage. Not just marriage for the sake of marrying, but a marriage that is healthy and worth being in.

Do you have a coach? As a single person desiring to be in a healthy marriage one day you should have a coach. Believe me we all need one. This person would act as your dating/ relationship "coach". Their purpose is very similar to the purpose of any coach, to guide, teach, and train you for optimum performance and of course the win, i.e. marriage.

Having a coach can open your eyes to things that you wouldn't normally see in the other person or in yourself. It will supply you with the wisdom and discernment that you may lack due to blinders that you have put on because of your desire to marry.

I know this concept of having a coach for your dating life is something that you are not used to, but if you find yourself frustrated with dating then you know that you have to change something.

I'm sure you have heard that God will not hold back any good thing from His children. It's true! He won't; so stop fearing that you will never get married. God really wants the best for you. Therefore, **He doesn't want you to keep dating sloppy seconds.** He wants you to have His first draft pick.

A coach can help you decipher if they are sloppy seconds or first picks.

Naomi and Ruth are two of my favorite Bible people. The relationship Ruth had with her mother-in-law, Naomi, was remarkable. Naomi was Ruth's coach and orchestrated her marriage to Boaz. Ruth trusted Naomi; therefore, she trusted that Boaz was a smart choice.

Paul is also another person who is great in the area of relationships (singleness and marriage). He provides us with relationship advice that will literally save our souls. Paul teaches us about fornication and the divide it causes in our connection with God.

Singles, you need a "Naomi" or a "Paul" in your life as your dating/ relationship coach. An adult who can lead and guide you in the right direction.

Don't think that dating in isolation is a good thing. It never is. I caution you not to enter into a relationship with someone unless a person you trust can vouch for their character.

There are reasons jobs will ask for recommendations. They want to talk to people who can speak to your work ethic. Similar to dating. You should be able to inquire about a person's life ethic before dating them. If no one can supply you with information then search other places. Having trusted godly people involved in your dating life is crucial to dating smart.

* * *

For many many years Christians have taken their dating cues and advice from BET, MTV, reality TV, and mainstream media. These portals have technically been our dating and relationship coaches. This has left us pregnant, diseased, wishing to be married, and wishing to be divorced. It's time that we do it God's way.

In the Bible there were various methods people used to choose their spouse. I personally like the method which involved a third person (or more) in the process. The third person wasn't just anyone; they were a trusted, godly, influential individual.

Yes, these marriages were arranged, but this is not to be confused with a forced marriage like some people think. It also should not be confused with the fact that they still had a choice although it was arranged.

An arranged marriage basically brings two people together and they choose if they want to stay together. A forced marriage is making two people marry with no choice at all.

Do you know a married couple that started dating because mutual friend(s) *hooked* them up? That was arranged.

Do you know two people that married because they ended up pregnant or because of a threat placed on their life? That's forced.

Don't believe that all biblical marriages were forced. They weren't and don't believe that they didn't have a choice because they did.

When Abraham wanted a wife for Isaac he sent Eleazar out to find Isaac a wife. Now, I don't want you to believe that this was a forced marriage because it wasn't. Isaac had a choice to marry whom he wanted and so did Rebekah.

Eleazar knew exactly what to look for in a wife for Isaac. Wouldn't that be great? You have someone searching for a spouse for you and they deliver the "perfect" one.

Eleazar knew Isaac personally since he had lived in Abraham's house with him all of his life. Furthermore, and oh so important, Eleazar was led by God. He saw Rebekah, tested her and decided that she was the one for Isaac. Rebekah happily accepted! (She could have declined.)

Read the text for yourself. You can find it in Genesis chapter 24. Eleazar came back with a woman for Isaac and she wasn't a *busted broke down chick* either. She was beautiful and she was worthy.

Similar to Isaac's arranged marriage so was Ruth's. Naomi was the person involved in hooking Ruth and Boaz up.

This is often viewed as the *Love Story* of the bible, and many women today want to find their *Boaz* and many men today want to find their *Ruth,* but very few use this method. Instead you find *Bozo* and *Ruthless.* People that cause hell and craziness in your life. They appear like the "one" on the surface but in actuality they are abusive verbally, emotionally and physically. They are the ones that had we conducted a background check on them we would have found out that they had six baby mama's, a drug addiction, a husband, a wife, and a whole lot of drama associated with them. (A background check can be as simple as Googling their name.) **Get that coach.**

Naomi was Ruth's coach. Every word Naomi told Ruth to do she did it. Ruth trusted Naomi to guide her in the right direction. Check her story out in the book of Ruth. Her story is so powerful she got her own book!

Naomi and Eleazar were devoted to God. They were godly, influential, trusting and discerning people, i.e. coaches. Ruth and Isaac weren't fearful that their *coaches* were going to pick someone ugly. They weren't fearful that they were going to pick someone that they weren't compatible with. In fact, Ruth and Isaac understood that marriage was about growing together in God.

You should also take a look at some people who had horrible dating habits and relationships. Like Samson in Judges 14-16. He had that lust demon for sure. Also look at Esau and the hell he caused his parents with his choice of women in Genesis 26:34 and 28: 6-9. Both of these men refused good direction.

Are you refusing good direction? Are you dating without a coach? Choose someone of the same sex to provide guidance as you date. You should have a genuine friendship with this person, as well as be able to trust them and know that they live a life for God filled with the Holy

Spirit. If they are married, their marriage should reflect God. This doesn't mean that their marriage will be perfect, but it means that Christ is the center of their marriage and you recognize that.

Like I said before, **dating can be deceptive** and many of us have been deceived. We all need that person who can help us to discern.

You must be transparent with your coach and feel comfortable revealing information about yourself that will help you date smart. Having a coach can help you weed out those no good *bustas* and save you sleepless nights.

Your coach should be able to spot a phony a mile away when you are all caught up in looks and material things. Be sure to take heed to the coach's insights because dating is deceptive. People will put their "best" foot forward just to impress you. **Find an excellent godly coach and listen to him or her.**

|NOTES|

Tip #9

FROM DATE TO MATE

I had a friend who expressed to me how much she liked this new guy she was dating. He was her "perfect" guy. As she continued to describe him to me she then said, "but he told me that he wouldn't marry me." If you could have seen my facial expression when she said that! I looked at the phone as if I were looking at her. Blinking my eyes rapidly as if I had something irritating in them.

This guy never wanted to be married and sadly she continued to date him. I advised her that it was not only a **bad idea** to continue in that relationship but also a set up for extreme heartache and pain.

I said it early on in the book: the purpose of dating is to get married. If you know that the one you are interested in is not interested in marriage then that is your cue to be out. *Peace. Deuces. Sayonara.* I don't care which vernacular you prefer but it all needs to indicate that you are departing with no intention to return again!

NO, YOU CANNOT CHANGE THEIR MIND. That is something that they will have to do on their own, and you shouldn't stick around for them to do so, because if they never do so then you are the one devastated.

Now, if they do change their minds about marriage then proceed from there, but NEVER wait around for them to do so. Waiting around for them to change their mind only makes you appear desperate as well as rob you of valuable time that you could be investing in someone that is willing to invest in you.

Too many of us stay in relationships hoping that the other person will marry us but in reality they won't. The longer we stay in those relationships the more difficult it becomes to get out. We become emotionally attached and eventually delusional. We convince ourselves that one day they will marry us, even when they have already said that they weren't interested in getting married. We think that we can change their mind and that's what we work towards.

How long have you stuck around trying to change their mind? It's time that you change your mind and leave.

When we are desperate we cannot think clearly; we do not function properly; we accept foolishness and sloppiness. Now, I like for my Sloppy Joes to be messy but I don't want a messy relationship and neither should you.

Ya'll, if the one you are with is not 100% committed then it's time for you to move out of that desperate neighborhood and into a place of confidence. Don't worry about packing your bags or calling the movers. Just leave with what you have on never to look back again. Believe me you will have no regrets. **Never stay where you aren't wanted.**

After a year of being in an exclusive relationship you should be moving toward marriage. Now this doesn't mean that you met them one year ago. It means that you have dated for one year. You should have known them or got to know them before you all became exclusive.

Do you remember the tip on becoming friends first?

If not refer back to tip #3. Do NOT neglect becoming friends first before moving into an exclusive serious relationship.

So, like I was saying before. After a year of being in an exclusive relationship you should be moving toward marriage. Let me tell you why I say that. Once you have dated for six months, you should know what kind of relationship you want to pursue. (Again, remember you should have known them and become friends with them before dating.) Too many people only look to pursue staying together for the benefits and not to wed.

It's important that ya'll **gain clarity** from each other where your relationship is headed. If ya'll have been honest with one another throughout the relationship then now should be no different. If you feel like you don't want to marry, then communicate that. If you want to get married, then communicate that too. The goal is to know where your relationship is headed and finding out if you both are on the same page.

Ladies, you don't have to convince him to marry you by nagging and begging him. If he wants to marry you he will.

Guys, if she says the relationship is moving too fast after being together for one year, then she doesn't want to marry you.

Staying in a relationship when you're not sure where it is headed is like walking in circles expecting to go somewhere.

Do you know people who wanted to get married but all they ever got was engaged? One person was eager to marry, but the other not so much. They would set a date but keep pushing it back the closer it got to that date.

Don't be fooled. He might propose and she may accept, but setting a date and following through with it is all that matters. If your date keeps changing then you may be getting played.

Not everyone is ready to get married and that is ok. If that is you then entering into a serious relationship is not for you; however, establishing genuine platonic friendships with the opposite sex may be. Just remember that you should never get physically involved and never make the other person believe that you are looking for more.

If you are in college, I recommend that you make friends instead of entering into serious relationships.. Instead hang out in groups, not as a couple but as friends just hanging out with other friends. A serious relationship at this point in your life can cause **many distractions, setbacks and set ups that you can't afford.**

There are too many STDs floating around and condoms aren't keeping them away. Did you know that you can still attract an STD while using a condom? Oh, yes you can. Google it. Condoms are not 100%. In fact, there are many condoms on the shelves that are defective. Furthermore, the more you have sex, especially with the same person, the less likely you are to use a condom.

Ask yourself is this a time for entering into a serious relationship?

Too many ladies are having abortions in college (and after) and too many guys pay for those abortions. Too many ladies get pregnant in college (and after) and too many guys get ladies pregnant.

Too many students enter into serious relationships only to break it off after one semester, and enter into another serious relationship with someone else.

The majority of the time serious relationships on college campuses involve sex. So, if you enter into a serious relationship over the course of your college journey, then most likely you will have had sex with multiple people, therefore associating you with hoe-ish behavior. No one wants the reputation of being the campus hoe.

Let me break down what a hoe is because we tend to apply this word to women only. A hoe is any person (yes male or female) who practices a life of fornication/adultery (including the way they present themselves). The Bible uses the terms whore (hoe is the shorter term), harlot and prostitute. It doesn't matter if a person has had sex one time or 100 times. Fornication/adultery is hoe-ish behavior. See we are conditioned to believe that hoe-ish behavior is sleeping around with a lot of different people or getting paid for sex, when in fact it is any kind of fornication and/or adultery no matter the number of partners or if we collect money.

In our culture it's deemed ok to have sex with the person you're in a relationship with and not be looked upon as a hoe. Whether in a relationship or not fornication is considered hoe-ish behavior.

I'm sure the wild college behavior of fornication or today's dating style is not the lifestyle you want to live to tell your children or grandchildren about. Therefore, I highly advise that if you are in college that you wait at least until you are ready to get married to date seriously.

The same advice should be applied for high school students. Exclusively dating in the 21st century at this age is not smart especially if your next step is college. However, hanging out as friends in groups with no relationship or dating expectations allows you to build healthy, platonic friendships. **Just because your friends are dating doesn't mean that you should.**

Dating is not a competitive sport as many often seek to make it. And I repeat. Just because your friends are dating someone doesn't mean that you have to date someone too. Don't allow that kind of pressure to overtake you.

It's dangerous to look at other people's relationships and be jealous, envious, and covetous. You have no idea what kind of hell that girl puts that dude through or what he puts her through. If we look at dating as something you have to do because everybody else is doing it then we will end up getting hurt and creating regrets. **Don't compete.**

As you mature in life (BTW maturity is not age related as much as it is your ability to discern and make better decisions), you should be able to know if a person is a person that you would want to marry without even dating them. Just watch them in different settings, around a crowd, how they present themselves on social media, what they're talking about, etc.

Dating smart is about making wise choices while dating. It's about the quality of the date not the quantity of dates. Dating smart is about the platonic friendships you make not the sex you take. Dating smart is about healthy interactions that will develop you to be a better person not a broken person. Dating smart is about discerning adequately who to date and who not to date. Dating smart is about moving towards marriage not baby mama or baby daddy status. **Dating smart will leave you satisfied with no regrets and propel you into the arms of your mate with confidence and surety.**

NOTES

Bonus Tip

Marriage

*T*oo often singles view dating as benefits (sex, living together, financial stability, etc.) without the commitment. Singles become so comfortable with this dating style that they will continue to stay in a relationship for 10 years, 20 years and beyond 30 years with the same person and never marry them.

The dating arena today has all the benefits of marriage without the commitment or the blessings of God. This kind of dating is careless dating which will cause for a careless marriage.

The purpose of dating is to get married. Whenever your time is it will come. Be sure to spend more time grooming yourself for the marriage and not just the wedding day. **Marriage is a commitment that God does not intend you to back out of.**

If you are dating someone and are considering marriage sit down with a marriage counselor as a couple and individually. You're not trying to find out if you two are compatible but if you as an individual are ready for marriage.

People don't divorce because they are incompatible. They divorce because both or at least one person isn't willing to continue in the marriage or seek the help they need in order to make the marriage work. Many people are compatible with multiple people but not every person is willing.

Marriage is not for the weak or the easily discouraged. It is for people who are serious and willing to endure tough times, enjoy great times, and grow together.

Don't go into a marriage with divorce as an option. Like Jesus said in Matthew 19:8 divorce was not an option when God ordained marriage. This isn't to say that you stay with an adulterous spouse or an abusive spouse, but it doesn't mean that you divorce them either. Separating for a period of time sometimes becomes a married couples' journey. During this time they seek professional help in order to come back together for the betterment of the marriage.

There are marriages that have surveyed adultery and abuse and these couples share their stories.

Ask yourself are you willing to work on even the toughest things like adultery.

Not all marriages go through adultery and abuse but you will go through some things that will make you want to say **"I don't" after saying "I do"**. Are you really ready to say "I do"?

With marriage comes the good, the bad, and the ugly. Those who date smart have more good in marriage; they are equipped to work in order to get over the bad, and they are willing to endure the ugly and turn it into being pretty.

As I was in the final stages of writing this book, I attended a marriage seminar at my church. There were married couples there, of course, as well as couples that were dating and couples that were engaged.

I want to share with you a few points that I gained

from the seminar.

The points are as follows:

- Marriage is a selfless act of serving entered into by two people who establish their commitment to be willing to work through all issues. *NOTE: It takes both husband and wife to work through issues in order to have a marriage worth living in.*
- There are no matches made in heaven. God doesn't write your name and their name in a heart on the front of a notebook or carve it into the tree of life. What He does do is give you wisdom to choose freely and provide you with the knowledge and understanding in order to be married. It is solely up to you and the one you date to work towards marriage or not. If you decide to marry it is then your decision as well to work to stay married.
- Marriage is a partnership not a dictatorship.
- Marriage is teamwork not individual work.
- Marriage will develop your character (even when you think it doesn't need developing) in order to be a better spouse.
- Marriage has ebbs and flows.
- Marriage is part of God's plan.

Of course there is so much more to be said about marriage, but that is for you to discover as you educate yourself on what marriage is. (This is a dating book not a marriage book.)

If you are not ready for marriage that is perfectly OK. If you never want to be married that is perfectly OK too.

|NOTES|

Conclusion

Hello New Me

When I adopted these tips to my life I dated less frequently. Before, I dated to get married but more so just to have something to do. Now, I date with a purpose. The purpose of marrying.

Does that mean I would tell a guy on the first date that I'm ready to marry him? Heck no! If a guy told me that on our first date that probably would be our last. That's one way to scare a person off; so, don't do that.

I date with a purpose, therefore I don't book a date with every guy that flirts with me or that I think is attractive. During the very first encounter (which is face to face) I decipher the guys intentions as much as possible through how he approaches me or how he responds to basic questions I may ask.

Now, I don't want you to think that I'm grilling the dude. I basically respond with a question based on his approach. So, if he approaches me and says: *I want to take you out this weekend.* I would respond by saying: *why would you want to take me out?* That leads to small talk which prompts more *Why* questions.

You can gain valuable information about a person based on their approach. Those few minutes of communication are key because they reveal green flags, yellow flags or red flags.

The green flag means good. The yellow flag means proceed with caution, if you proceed at all. The red flag means stop. Don't go any further.

Are you paying attention to the flags or are you ignoring them?

Lately though, I have been on the fence about marriage. What do you mean Linda? Well let me explain. When I was a teen and in my earlier 20's I focused on being married. That's not so much the case now.

This doesn't mean that I don't think there aren't good men out there. The world has plenty of - not just good men but great men.

So, women stop bashing all men based off a few men. And guys stop bashing all women based off a few women.

Remember you attract who you are. If you are attracting *pigeons* and *scrubs* than look at why you may be attracting those kinds of people.

So, like I was saying, these days I'm not so focused on getting married. Therefore, I'm on the fence with deciding if I want to be married at all. I'ma be honest. I'm enjoying where my life is at this point.

Does this mean that I will never marry? I don't know. I guess it all depends on how I feel later in life, but right now I'm loving my single life and I can't imagine my life being any other way.

Does this mean that I think I'm an "independent" woman with the attitude of *I don't need a man*? NO, not at all.

Ladies, if you have this attitude and want to be

married, go back to tip #1 right now.

I genuinely thank God for my singleness and I'm sure there are other singles out there who may feel the same way as I do.

Now, the days that I do think about one day marrying I contemplate if I would be a willing wife. Ya'll, I'm still fixing myself! Ya girl right here loves to be in control and love things to go her own way. I admit it! This is something that I recognize about myself and there are other people out there who are the same way (married and single) but you don't like to admit it.

Well, I thank God! I have improved significantly over the years. I'm less controlling and I have less of a desire to have everything go my way only. I've found that not only is it detrimental to any dating relationship but also friendships, business partners, parenting and any relationship in general.

I am in no rush to marry right now; therefore I am in no rush to be in a relationship either.

Now, you may be in a rush to get married. Question: *Why*? I'm not trying to convince you to never get married. I'm trying to help you understand why you want to be married. Are you rushing to marry because you want children? Are you rushing to marry because you want to have "legal" sex? Are you rushing to marry because you're trying to cover up a pregnancy? Why are you in a rush?

It doesn't matter what your answers are to these questions. What does matter though, is that you marry to glorify God.

Adopting these tips in your dating life will be life-changing. More importantly operating by Biblical principles will be rewarding. In order to reap the best reward though, you must choose wisely.

See, God created us with the freedom of choice. You

weren't just dealt a hand. You chose your hand in dating. Your dating life is what it is because you chose it to be that way. You can also choose it to be better.

We choose who we will date and we choose who we will marry. Let your choice be one that does not have you dating *CRAZY*.

Go and be a new you and date smart.

|NOTES|

Appendix 1

| My list |

This list is in no particular order.

- Authentic, ongoing relationship with God through being filled with the Holy Spirit
- Pure (Purity in mind and lifestyle)
- Honesty
- Trustworthy
- Faithful
- Committed/ Ability to Endure
- Godly Wisdom/ Discernment
- Funny/ Humor
- Look good in my eyes
- Passion for career/ Fulfilling dreams/ Vision for life
- Confident in who God made him to be
- Romantic/ Know how to have a good time/ Live not just exist
- Supportive of my ideas and career
- Leader/ Spiritual Leader/ Friend
- Help me to become a better person/ Inspiring/

Encouraging
- Willingness to continue learning and growing for the betterment of self and for the sake of the relationship
- Educated/ Continuing education (This doesn't only mean a college degree, but it means that he will read and research for the sake of gaining more knowledge.)
- Responsible/ Accountable for his actions and taking ownership when he is wrong
- Financial wisdom and practices for the present and future (i.e., 401K/ 403B or equivalent)
- Insurance: Life; Health; Car
- Set and achieve personal goals; career goals; etc.
- Content while striving for better

Appendix 2

Me, Myself and I

- No sex (including kissing and sensual touch) - Non negotiable
- No shacking up - Non negotiable
- No co-signing - Non negotiable
- No long term dating relationships, including long term engagements - Non negotiable
- Take separate cars on dates - negotiable
- Don't even ask me to have more babies...lol...- negotiable

Workbook

90 Day Transformation

During the next 90 days commit to completing this workbook. You are free to set your own schedule and work at your own pace. Remember this: You can only choose to change yourself and no one else.

In this workbook you will find a series of questions to answer based on the tips. Also included are guidelines to help assist with your transformation, such as: scripture to study.

Your success at completing this workbook depends on your commitment. Let go of excuses in order to embrace growth.

Questions:

<u>Me and God</u>

Do I desire to have a godly character?   YES   NO

What does that look like? _____

_____

_____

Where do I need to commit or improve upon my commitments to God?

_____

_____

_____

Am I where I want to be in my relationship with God? If not, how can I get where I want to be? Do I even know where I want to be?

_____

_____

_____

Who are my friends that I can call on for prayer, clarity of the Bible, or godly advice?

_____

_____

_____

Self-reflection

What are my hobbies or what do I enjoy doing?

_____

_____

_____

How can I be a better person?

_____

_____

_____

Who do I need to cut ties with that is or may be hindering my growth in the area of: purity, relationship with God, career, etc.? Delete numbers, unfollow on social media, etc.

_____

_____

_____

What did I appreciate about my past relationships?

_____

_____

_____

What didn't I appreciate about my past relationships?

_____

_____

_____

What were some red flags I ignored in the past?

_____

_____

_____

What am I doing differently or will I do differently in relationships from here on out?

_____

_____

What grudges, if any, am I holding from past relationships? How can I release these grudges so they will not inflict my future marriage?

_____

_____

_____

Purity

Is practicing purity important to me?   YES   NO

What (who) are some things or people in my life that are keeping me from practicing purity?

_____

_____

_____

What are the precautions I will implement so that I can practice purity?

_____

_____

_____

Single Parent

What are my goals as it relates to parenting?

_____

_____

_____

How do I plan to achieve those goals?

_____

_____

_____

How do I plan to teach my child(ren) about dating?

_____

_____

Do I know what it takes to have two families become one (i.e. blended family)?   YES   NO   NOT REALLY

(Check out: *Blending to Make It: Ingredients for a Successful Blended Family* by Dr. Duane E. Mangum)

How can I co-parent with my child(ren)'s mother/father for the betterment of our child(ren)?

_____

_____

_____

Do I put my child's mother/father down? YES   NO

How can I stop putting down my child's mother/father?

_____

_____

_____

How can I encourage team work with my child(ren)'s mother/father?

_____

_____

_____

Who would my child(ren) select as a mentor or who would I select as a mentor for my child(ren)? (This should be someone that your child(ren) is/are comfortable with and that you are comfortable with.)

_____

_____

_____

Dating & Marriage Insights

What are my fears about marriage? Why do I have these fears? How will I overcome them?

_____

_____

_____

What are some personal commitments that I can establish now for how I will function in my future marriage?

_____

_____

_____

Do I desire to have a godly marriage?   YES   NO

What might that look like?

_____

_____

_____

Who can I ask to be my dating coach (same gender)?

_____

_____

_____

Who can I ask to be my accountability partner (same gender)?

_____

_____

_____

What do I need my accountability partner to hold me accountable to?

_____

Things To Do:

Pray

For the next 90 days say this prayer (you are welcome to add to it): Father, show me how you need me to change in order to become a better person. Download, from you to me, your wisdom, knowledge and understanding so that I will not get caught up, hooked on or involved in CRAZY dating relationships. Help me to understand that my identity and my worth are defined by YOU and not a relationship status. Let my choices reflect your Word and not my lust or brokenness. Fix me Jesus. Allow me to be open to receiving your instructions. Teach me how to be a spouse and as you teach me please teach my future spouse. In the name of Jesus.

Volunteer

Occupy your time with volunteering at least 3 times during your 90 Day Transformation. You should choose your volunteer venue based on your talents, gifts and passions. You want to enjoy this experience. Don't let the day go by without connecting with a volunteer coordinator of your choice.

Scripture

It's imperative that you meditate and study scripture during your 90 Day Transformation. You should schedule a daily time with no distractions. Meditate and study the book of Proverbs. Don't rush through it. Create a personal reading plan that will allow you to spread out the chapters over the next 90 days. Take notes and reflect on it.

|NOTES|

Linda is The Woman's Life Coach. If you are looking to get your life in order, gain clarity, or move forward in life but need some help doing so connect with Linda today. She would love to help you. You can contact her via her website.

Subscribe to Linda's blog and follow her for more great tips, reads and conversations.
www.LindaDLowe.com
Twitter: @LLivingthelife
FB: https://www.facebook.com/livingthelifeministry (Linda D. Lowe)

Please tweet your most favorite line in the book. Don't forget to tag Linda @LLivingthelife.

To read the full story "The Search" go to Linda's website. Click Today's Word and search The Search.
www.LindaDLowe.com

www.ingramcontent.com/pod-product-compliance
Lightning Source LLC
Chambersburg PA
CBHW071717040426
42446CB00011B/2108